Original publication: "Notopísanka 3"
Author: Eva Šašinková, M.M., Ph.D., M.B.A.
Illustrations: Mgr. Kateřina Kovářová
Original graphic design: Lumír Kaděra
Original publisher: Czech Music Edition, Prague, Czech Republic, 2023
Website: www.hudebni-publikace.cz
Copyright: Eva Šašinková, M.M., Ph.D., M.B.A.
Original Czech version ISBN: 978-80-908706-8-0

English adaptation: "Clefi's Music Workbook 3"
Illustrations: Mgr. Kateřina Kovářová
Translation, adaptation, and graphic design: Roman Placzek, D.M.A.
Publisher: BumbleBeeNotes™ Music Publishing, Manlius, NY, USA, 2024
Catalog number: cbbn002-wb-005
Website: www.bumblebeenotes.com
Copyright: BumbleBee Notes™ Inc. Music Corporation
ISBN: 979-8-9919035-4-7

What's Inside:

Musical clefs
Bass clef
Octaves & octave transposition symbols
Notes & clefs on musical staff
The third octave and its notes in bass clef
Songs in the third and second octaves
The second octave - its notes, C major scale
The fourth octave's notes in bass clef
Duration of note and rests
Time signature

Dear friends of the bass clef,

My warmest greetings to all of you who play the piano, harp, or any bass instrument. As you know, children's songbooks are all written in the treble clef. But who knows the bass clef as well as the treble clef? My friends who play the violoncello, double bass, and bassoon were saddened not to find activities and tasks in the bass clef. And the pianists and harpists who use both clefs joined them as well. Therefore, this third music workbook is especially for you, my dear bass friends. Fun quizzes, tasks, and even the songs in this book are all in the bass clef. Enjoy your bass music workbook!

Yours, Clefi

Similar to "Clefi's Little Notebook," this book presents a collection of enchanting folk songs from the rich Czech folklore tradition, designed for music education. To accurately utilize their intended purpose, each song requires accurate adaptation and translation into English, which would take up more space than these volumes can accommodate without disrupting their intended design. Therefore, we are offering a standalone "Clefi & Notelina's Songbook," featuring all the songs from all nine volumes of Clefi's New Music Education School series, along with accurately and sensibly translated and adapted English lyrics.

Musical Clef

The **musical clef** is the **first musical symbol** on the **staff**. It determines the **position** and the **pitch** of the **notes** on the staff.

The treble or violin clef and the bass clef are the most commonly used clefs.

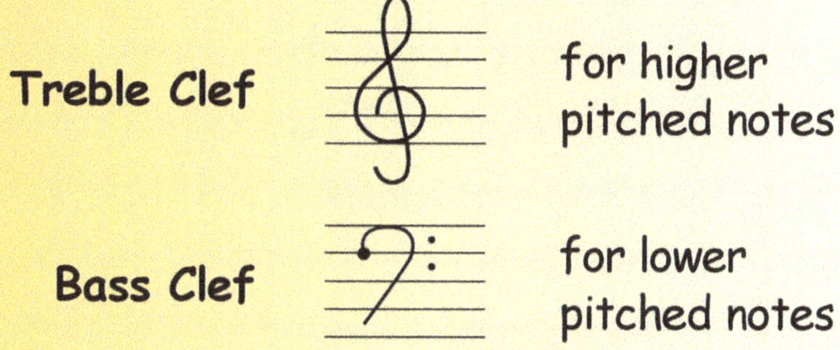

Treble Clef — for higher pitched notes

Bass Clef — for lower pitched notes

E Color the leaves with the **bass clef yellow** and the ones with the **treble clef green**.

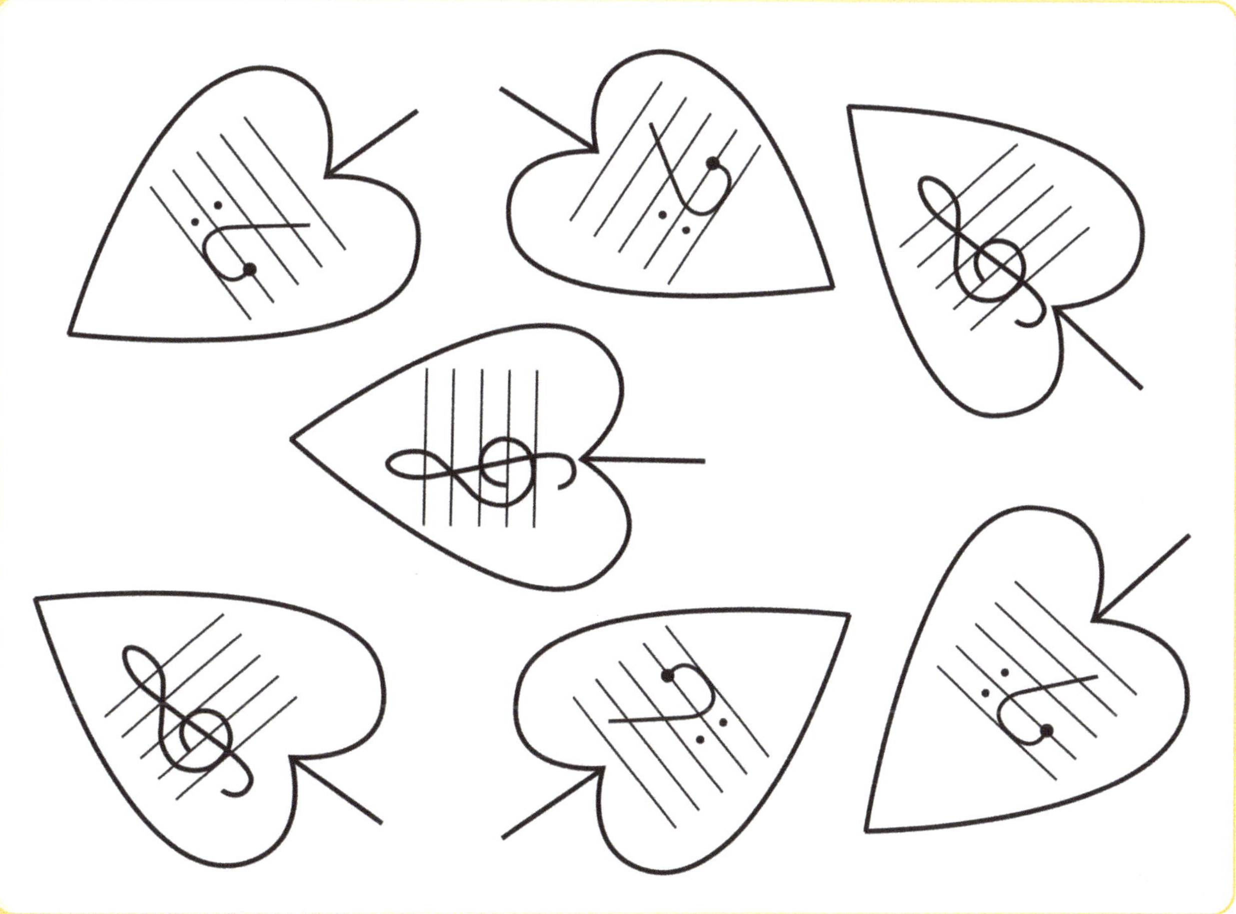

Octaves

Clefi's Little Notebook, pg. 35; Clefi's Music Notebook 1, pg. 4

The **primary tone row** has **seven** tones: C, D, E, F, G, A, and B. These tones are played on the **white keys** of the **keyboard**. They **repeat** in the **same order** at **different heights**. Each repeated group of the primary tones is called an **octave**. Each octave has its own **designated number**.

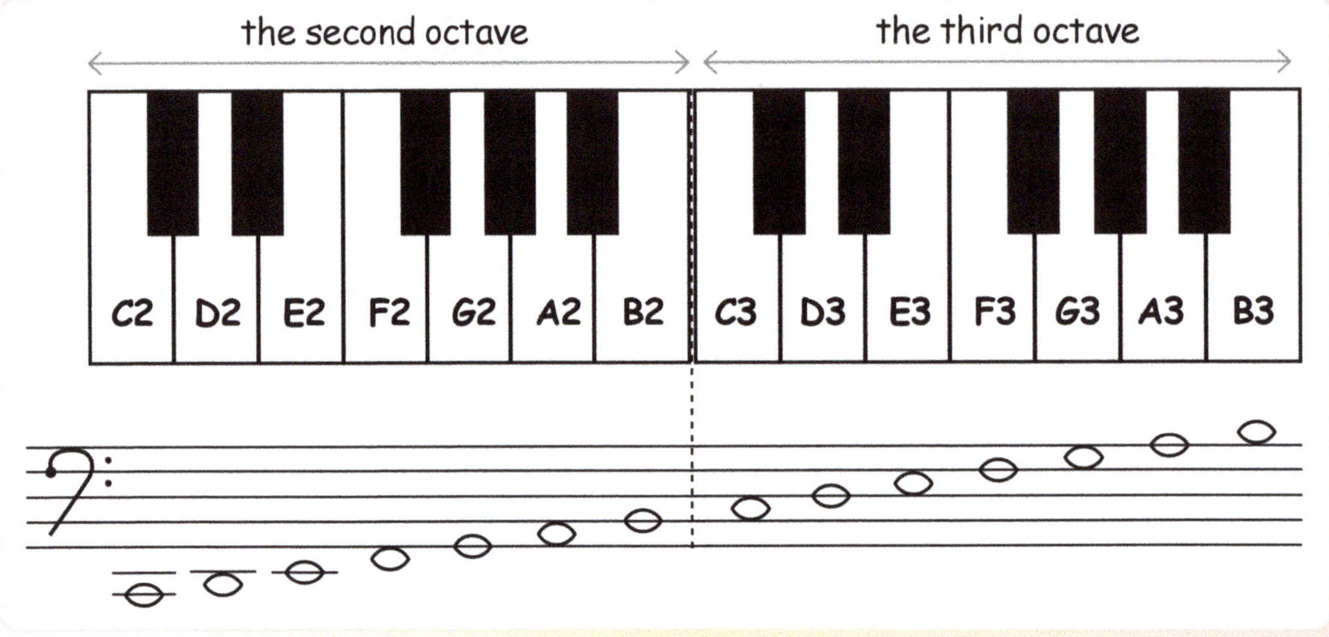

E Find the **tones** below on the **keyboard** and **connect** them with their **appropriate octave**.

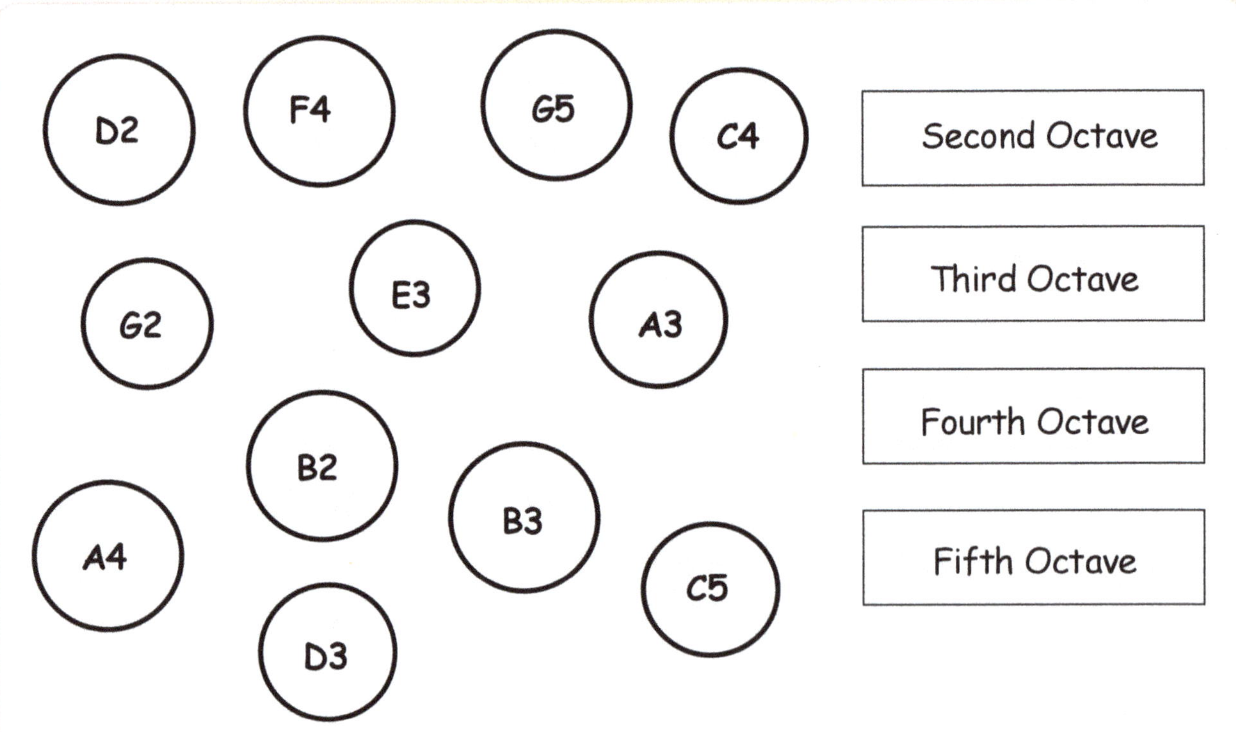

To keep all the repeated tones **organized**, the tones contained in each octave have their **octave's number**. A **higher number** means a **higher-positioned octave** on the **keyboard** and the **staff**.

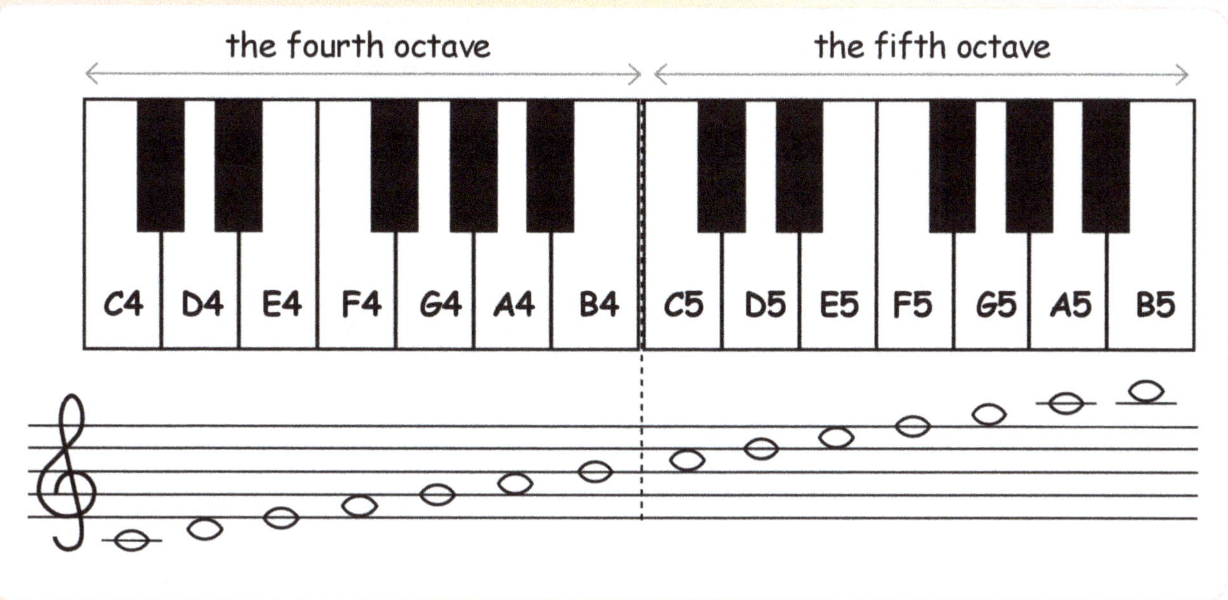

E **Color** the box with the **lower tone** of each **pair**. Use various colors.

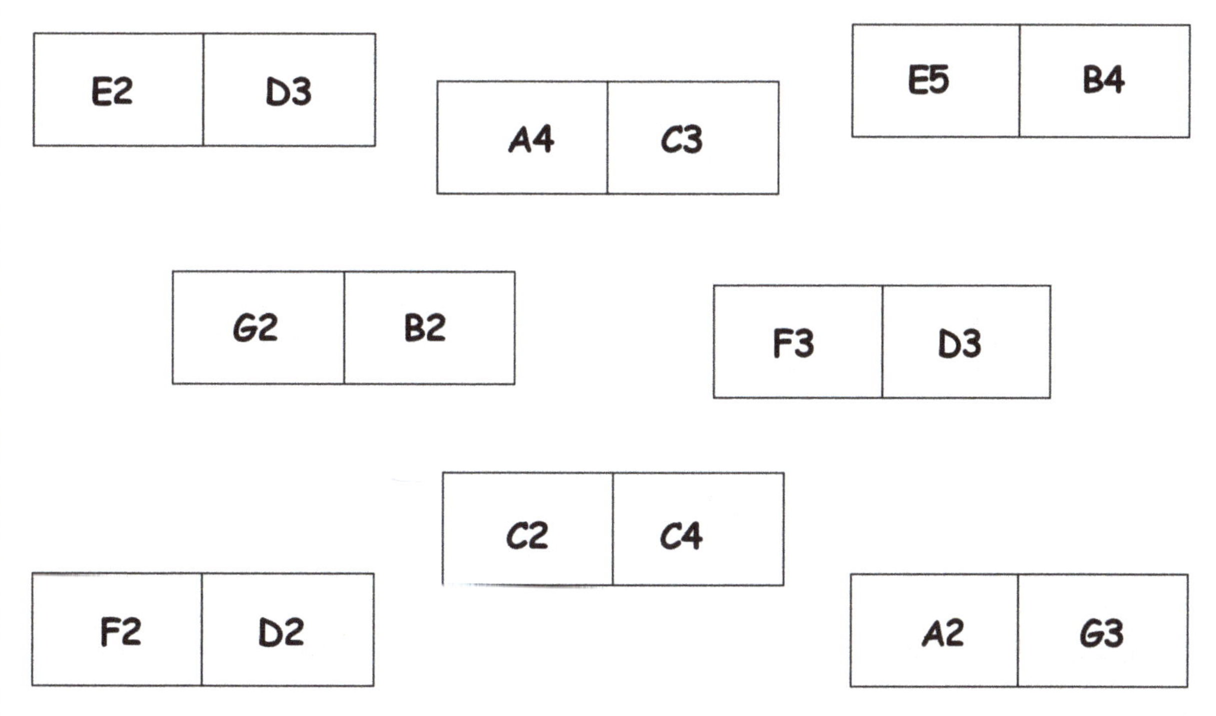

Notes & Musical Staff

Clefi's Little Notebook, pg. 18 - 21

The **musical staff** has **five** lines and **four** spaces.
When **writing** the **notes** onto the **musical staff**, we place them:

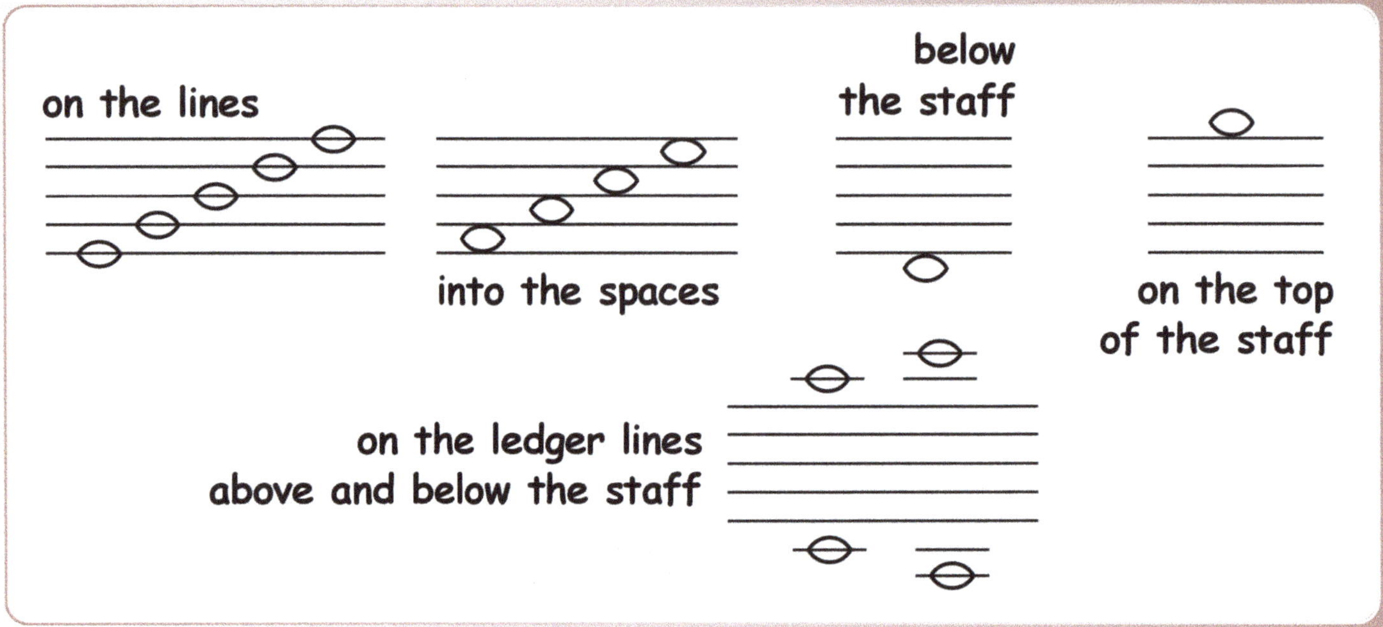

on the lines

below
the staff

into the spaces

on the top
of the staff

on the ledger lines
above and below the staff

E Write **half notes** according to the **descriptions**. Mind the stems!

on the 2nd line

below the staff

in the 3rd
space

on the 5th line

in the 1st
space

on the 4th line

on the first
ledger line
above the staff

on the second
ledger line
below the staff

Musical Clefs on Musical Staff

Clefi's Little Notebook, pg. 22

Every **clef** has a **precisely designated place** on the **musical staff**.

The **treble clef**, also known as the **violin clef**, begins by encircling the **second line**, where the note **G4** lives. That's why it's also called the **G clef**.

The **bass clef** starts on the **fourth** line and elegantly embraces the **entire staff. Two dots** behind it highlight the home to the note **F3**. That's why it is also called the **F clef**.

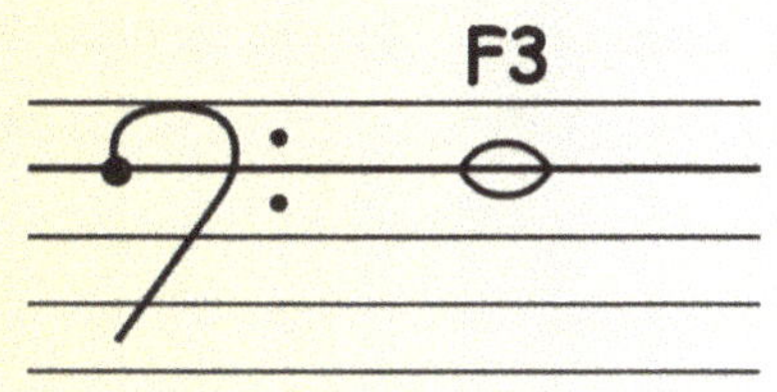

E Circle the **correctly** placed **bass** clefs.

Can you tell which **instruments** are associated with the **bass clef** and which with the **treble clef**? Draw the **appropriate clefs** in the **boxes** next to each instrument and then **color** the **instruments**. *Clefi's Musical Instrumeents*

Bass Clef

The **bass clef** starts on the **fourth line**.

- Make a **dot** on the **fourth line**; this is your starting point. Then, **draw** a nice **arch** stretching from the **fourth** to the **fifth line**. Practice it.

- Continue with a **line downward** to the **left**, extending all the way to the **center** of the **first space** (below the second line). Practice steps one and two.

- Mark **two dots** behind the clef: one in the **center** of the **fourth space** and the other in the **center** of the **third space**. Practice drawing the whole clef.

Third Octave

Clefi's Music Notebook 1, pg. 4 and 6

The notes of the **third octave** on the staff in the **bass clef**:

bass clef
F clef

C3 D3 E3 F3 G3 A3 B3

On the **middle line**, **D3** lives merrily
The **fourth line** is **F3**'s given place
There, the **bass clef** guards its family
With **dots** behind in the **third** and **fourth space**

C3 in the **second space** is blooming
Making sure all notes are well and sound
And **A3** that all instruments is tuning
On the **fifth line** now can be found

E Draw the **bass clef** and the **primary tones** in the **third octave**.

C3 D3 E3 F3 G3 A3 B3

E Do you recognize the **notes** from the **poem above**? **Name** all of them on the **dotted lines** below the staffs.

In the bass clef, the notes **C3, E3,** and **G3**
live in the **spaces 2, 3,** and **4.**

E Write the **half notes** above their **names**. Mind the **stems!**

In the bass clef, the notes **D3, F3,** and **A3**
live on the **lines 3, 4,** and **5.**

E Write the **half notes** above their **names**. Mind the **stems,** and do not
forget that the note **D3** can have stem placed **both ways.**

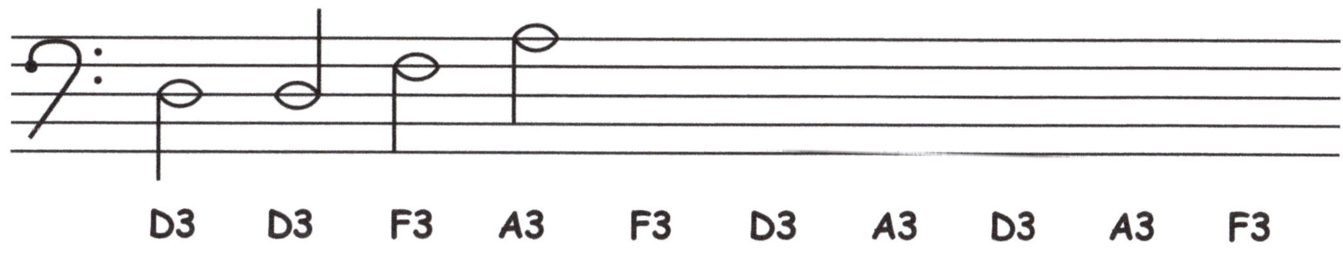

E Complete the quarter notes by **adding** their **stems. Circle** the notes on the
lines, then **name** all the **notes.**

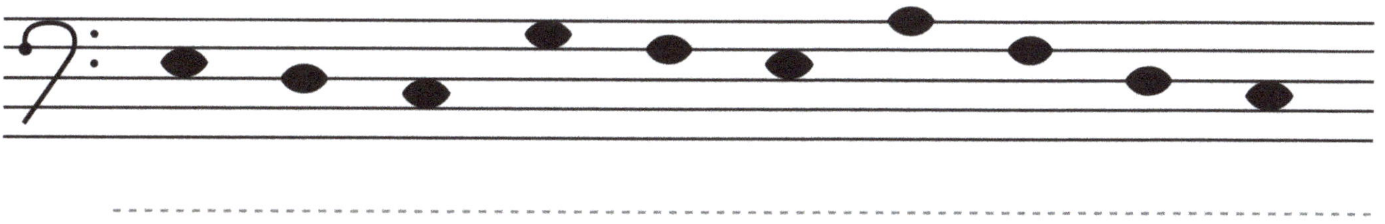

E Learn to **sing** the song using the **names** of the **notes.** Do you recognize it?
(*Clefi's Little Notebook,* page 52) **Circle** the **notes** in **spaces** in **blue.**

Notes C3 and D3

Clefi's Music Notebook 1, pg. 6

*When notating **eighth notes**, we must pay attention to the **placement of stems and flags**.* 

In the **bass clef**, the note **C3** sits in the **second space**.

♩ = 1 beat = the quarter note   ♪ = 1/2 beat = the eighth note

E Write the **C3 quarter** and **eighth** notes according to the values indicated below the staff.

| 1 | ½ | 1 | ½ | 1 | ½ | 1 | ½ | 1 | ½ |

In the **bass clef**, the note **D3** sits in the **third, the middle line**.

E Practice drawing the **D3 quarter** and **eighth** notes with stems and flags in **both directions**

𝅗𝅥 = 2 beats = the half note   ♩ = 1 beat = the quarter note

E Fill in the **names** of the **notes** and the **number of beats**.

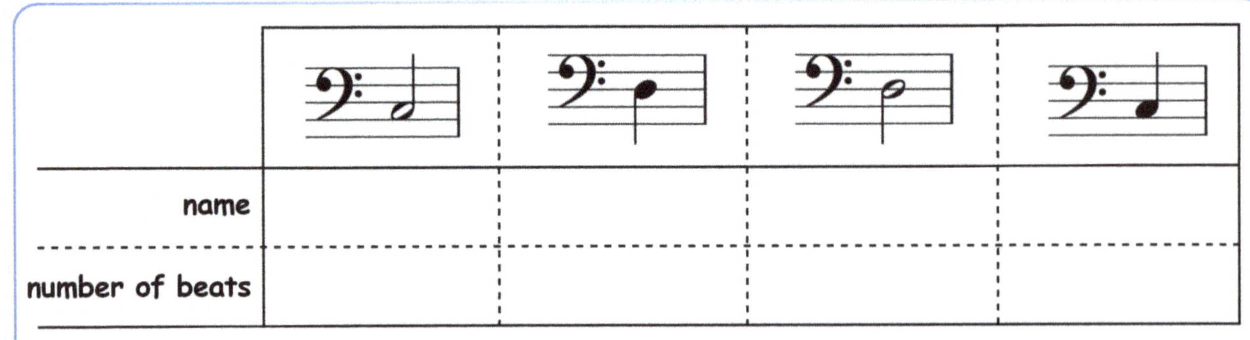

name			
number of beats			

Notes E3, F3, and G3

Clefi's Music Notebook 1, pg. 6

In the **bass clef**, the note E3 sits in the **third space**.

E Practice drawing the **quarter** and **eighth notes** E3.

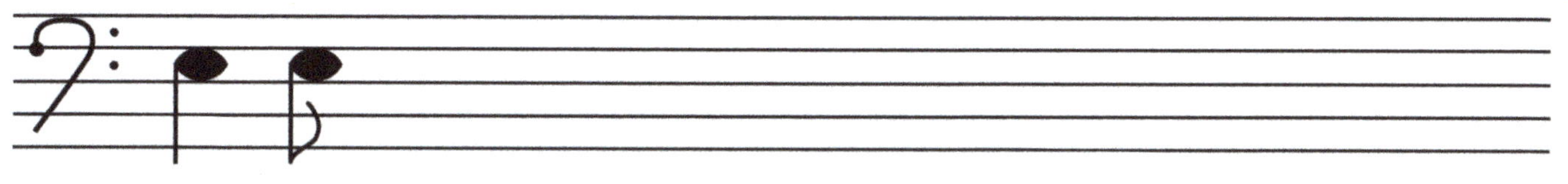

In the **bass clef**, the note F3 sits on the **fourth line**.

E Practice drawing the **quarter** and **eighth notes** F3.

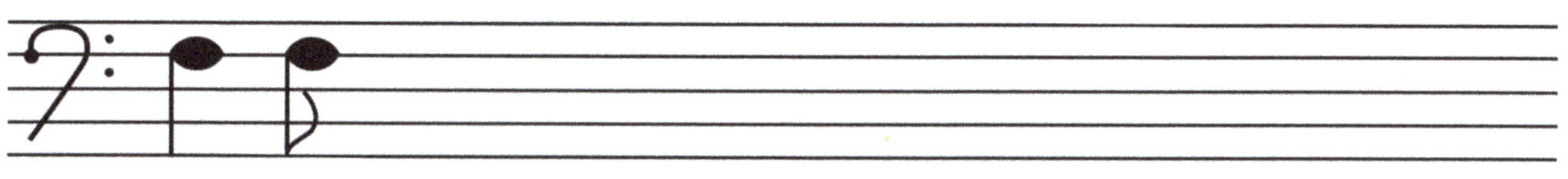

In the **bass clef**, the note G3 sits in the **fourth space**.

E Practice drawing the **quarter** and **eighth notes** G3.

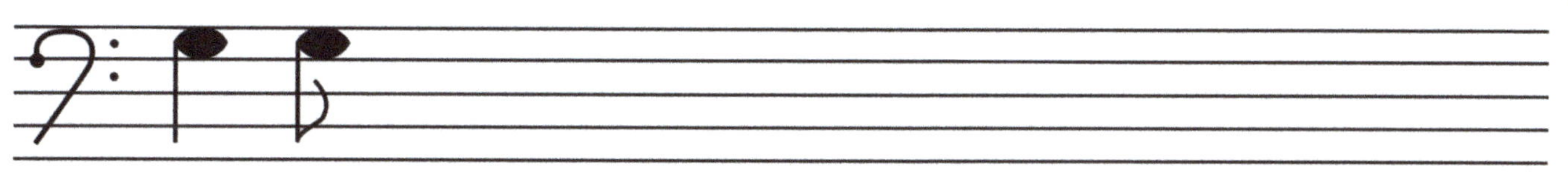

E Learn the song "The Mean Bagpiper" from Clefi's Songbook in *Clefi's Little Notebook* on page 55. **Write** the **names** of all the **notes** on the **dotted line** below the staff.

Notes A3 and B3

Clefi's Music Notebook 1, pg. 6

In the **bass clef**, the note **A3** sits on the **fifth line**.

E Practice drawing the **quarter** and **eighth notes A3**.

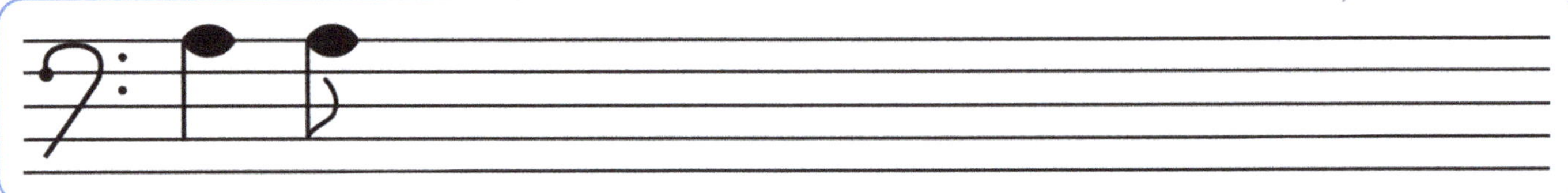

In the **bass clef**, the note **B3** sits on the **top of the staff**.

E Practice drawing the **quarter** and **eighth notes B3**.

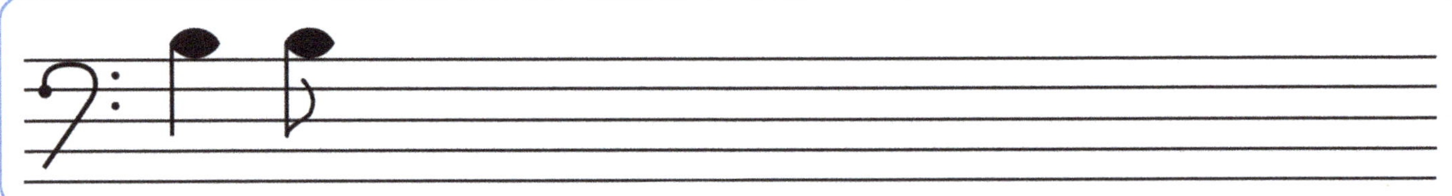

E Look at the first part of the song "Hey-ho, Little Sheep" from Clefi's Songbook in *Clefi's Little Notebook* (page 56) and **circle** all the **notes** that **do NOT belong** to the **third** octave.

Copy **measures** with the notes **B3**.

E Fill in the **missing notes** of the **primary tone row**.

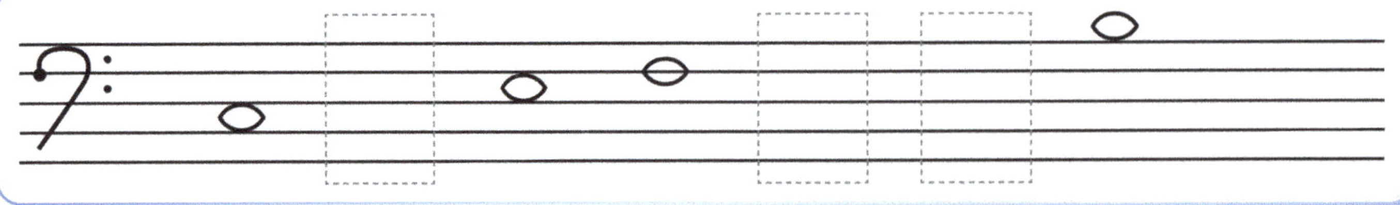

Notes From C3 to C4

B3 is the **highest note** of the **third octave**. Above B3 is C4, the **first** and **lowest note** of the **fourth octave**.

E Write the **names** of all the **notes** on the staff on the dotted line below.

The C major Scale In the Third Octave

C3   D3   E3   F3   G3   A3   B3   C4

E Draw the **bass clef** and write the **C major scale** according to the example.

C3   D3   E3   F3   G3   A3   B3   C4

E Draw the **bass clef** and write the **quarter notes** according to their **names** below the staff.

C3   E3   G3   B3   D3   F3   C4   G3   D3

Notes With the Beam

Clefi's Little Notebook, pg. 24

If **several notes** with **flags** next to each other belong to one **rhythmical phrase**, we can **connect** them with the **beam**.

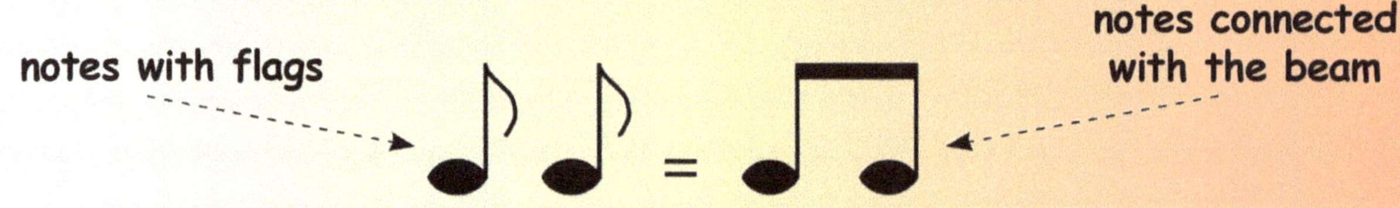

E Practice drawing **notes** with a **flag** and **notes connected** by the **beam**.

E Draw the **bass clef** and write the **eighth notes** according to the **names**. The **notes** in the **bracket** connect using the **beam**.

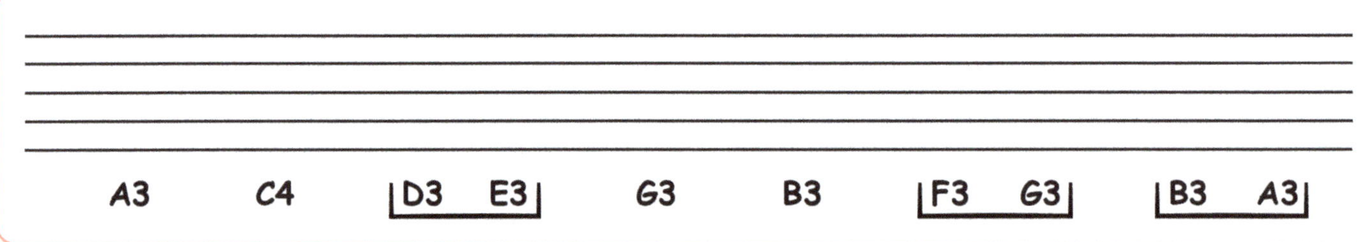

E Fill in the **values** of the **notes**.

half note				

Little Review
Duration of Notes & Rests

E Write the **number** of **beats** of the shown **notes** and **rest** into the boxes.
Color the **sections** of the picture with the **assigned colors**.

Red = the **whole** notes and rests

Blue = the **half** notes and rests

Yellow = the **quarter** notes and rests

Green = the **eighth** notes and rests

Time Signature

Clefi's Little Notebook, pg. 30 and 31

On the staff, the **time signature - meter - sits next to the clef.**
The meter shows the **number of beats** in a **measure** and the **beat value.**

two-four, 2/4 measure
has two beats;
the quarter note is
the beat

three-four, 3/4 measure
has three beats;
the quarter note is
the beat

Four-four, 4/4, or otherwise known as common measure,
has four beats; the quarter note is the beat.

E Connect the **name** of the **measure** with the **correct time signature.**

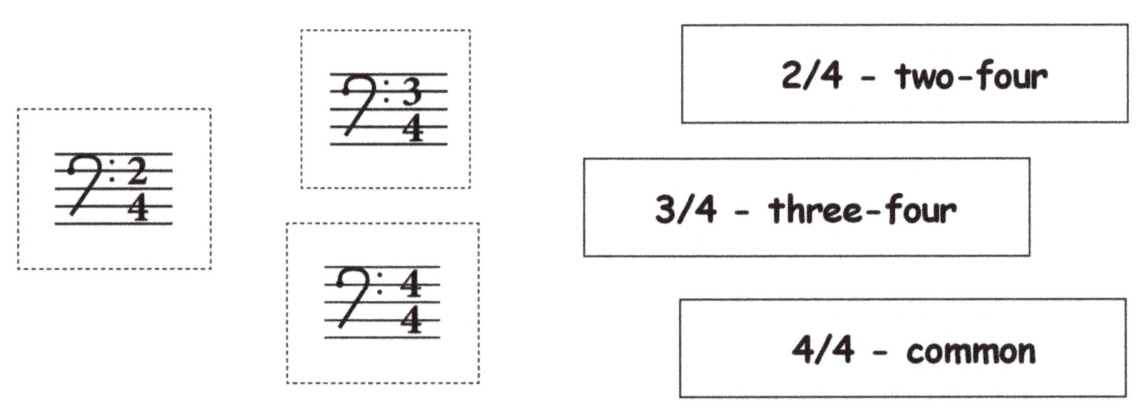

E Write the **number of beats** per **measure** in the top box and draw the **note** representing the **beat** in the bottom one. Then, **name the measures.**

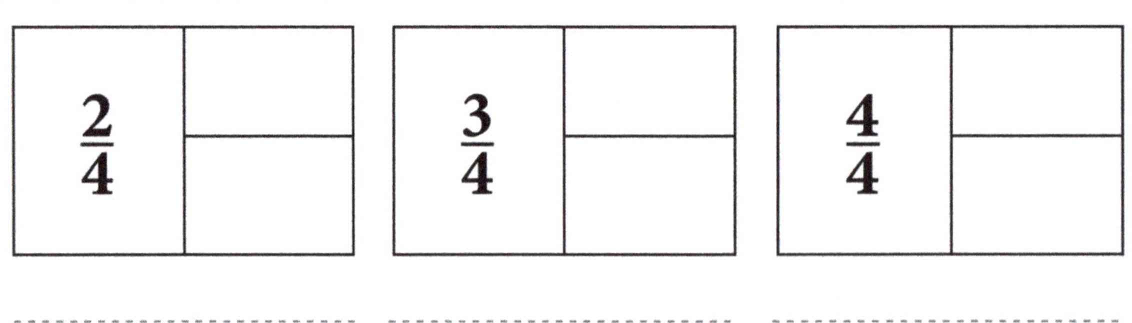

The **four-four** time signature is also known as the **common meter**.
We can mark it with **numbers 4/4** or with the capital letter **C**.

E Practice writing of the **four-four** and **common** time signatures.
Pay attention to the **placement** of the **numbers** and the letter **C**.

E Practice writing of the **two-four** and **three-four** time signatures.
Pay attention to the **placement** of the **numbers**.

E Place the **time signatures** in the boxes following the clef based on the
number of **beats** per **measure**.

a)

b)

c)

d)

Songs in Third Octave

E Clap the **rhythm** of the new song "LittleFish," then **sing** it using the **names** of the **notes**.

Clefi & Notelina's Songbook, pg. 40

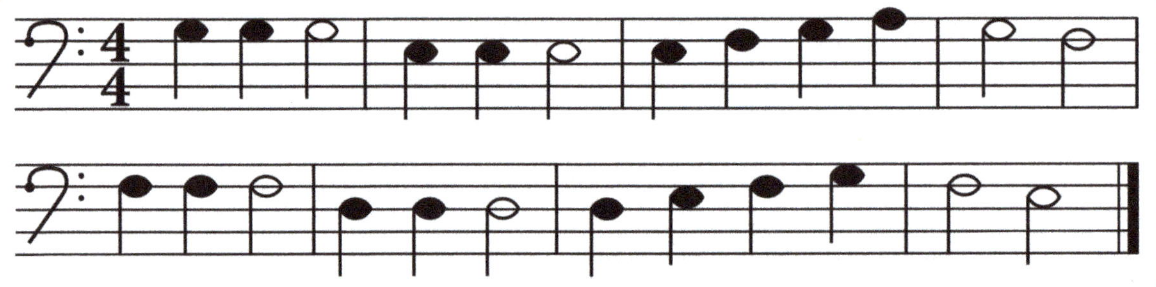

E In each section below, find the **measures** in the song above a **fill** in the **measure** that **follows** it. **Number** each section in **correct order** to put the song back together.

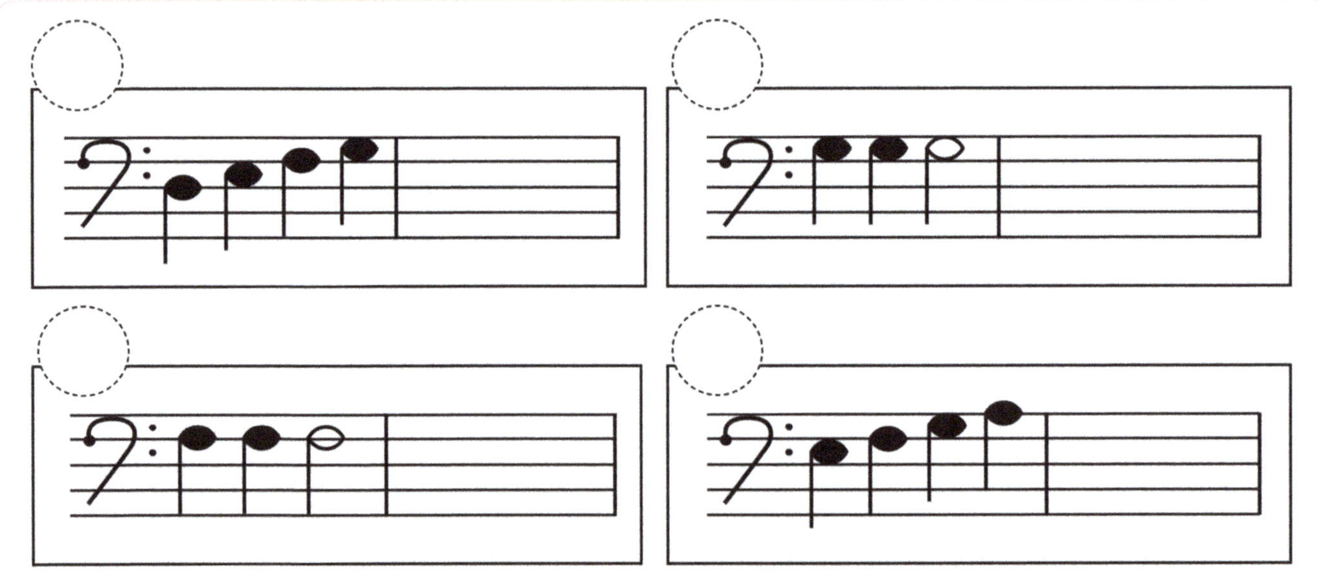

E In the rhythmic transcription of the song above, **find** and circle the **six** **notes** with **wrong rhythmic values**.

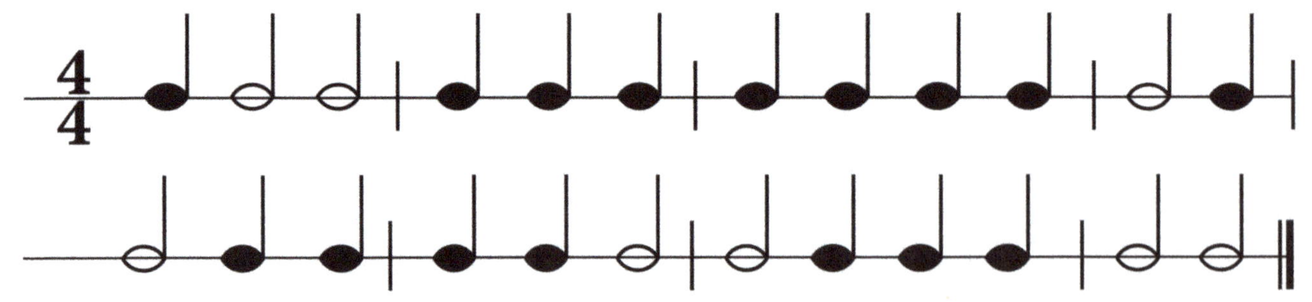

Some songs start with the **melodic tonic fifth chord**. The **tonic fifth cord** is built from the **first**, **third**, and **fifth degrees** = notes of a **scale**.

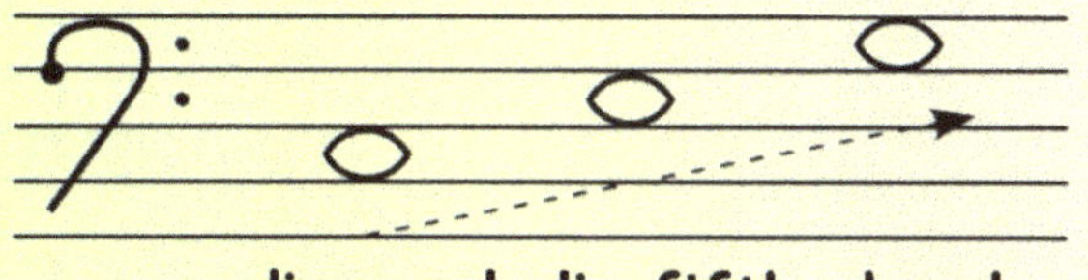

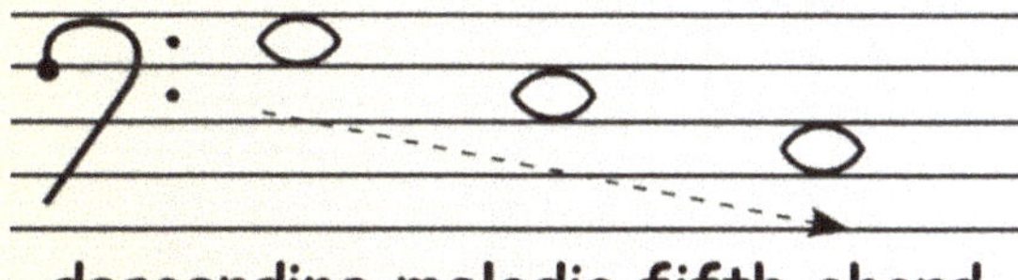

E In the song "Little Sheep, Not a Peep," find a **melodic tonic fifth chord** and **name** all its **notes**.

E Look up the **song** about a bass behind a stove on page 30 of *Clefi's Musical Instruments*. **Transpose** the song from the **treble clef** to the **bass clef** and **circle** all **ascending** and **descending melodic fifth chords**.

Clefi & Notelina's Songbook, pg. 28

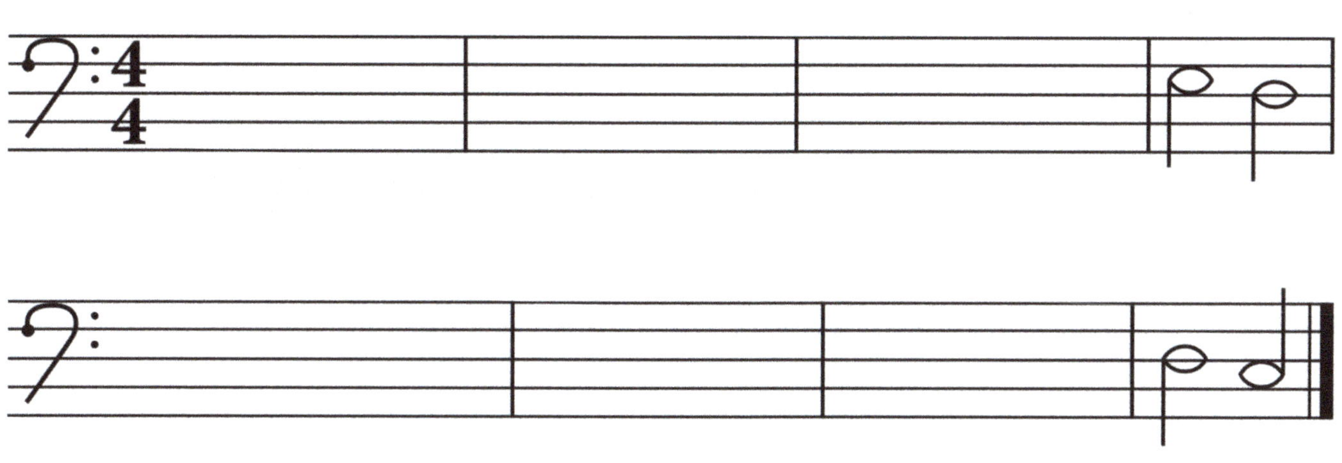

Second Octave

The notes of the **second octave** on the staff with the **bass clef**:

bass clef
F clef

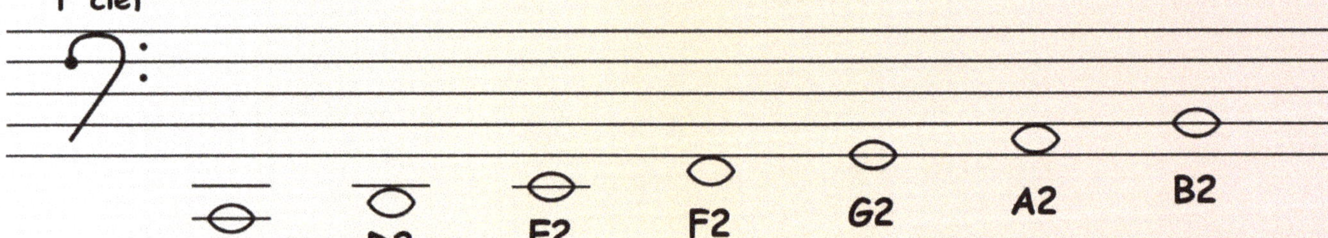

C2 needs **two ledger lines**
  right **below the staff**.
E2, on the other hand,
  says **one** is just enough.

G and B, both number **2**,
  each took one bottom **line**.
C, E, G, and B, all **2**,
  love their **lines** just fine.

E Can you identify the **notes** below? Use the **poem** as a **guide**.

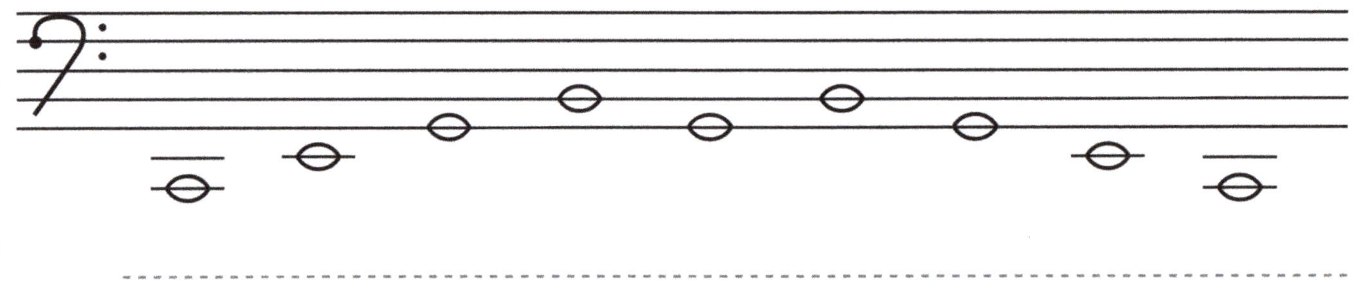

E The notes G2, A2, and B2 live within the staff. Copy the **notes**.

The notes **C2**, **D2**, **E2**, and **F2** are positioned **below** the **staff**. It's essential to **place** the **ledger lines accurately**, ensuring they are **spaced** the same as the **lines** on the **staff**.

E Learn to write the whole and half notes **C2** and **E2**.

Use the **dotted lines** to draw the correct **ledger lines**.

E Learn to write the whole and half notes **D2**. Draw the **bass clef** and alter between the **whole** and **half D2** notes.

E Learn to write the quarter and eight notes **F2**. Draw the **bass clef** and alter between the **quarter** and **eighth F2** notes.

E Draw the **bass clef**, write the **4/4** time signature, and fill in the **half notes** as indicated by their **names** below the staff. Mark the **bar lines**.

B2   A2   G2   F2   E2   D2   C2   D2   E2   F2

E Draw the **bass clef** and mark the **4/4 meter**. Write the **half notes** according to their names and fill in the **bar lines**.

G2   E2   C2   A2   F2   D2   B2   G2   A2   C2

E Draw the **bass clef** and the **2/4 key signature**. Write the **eighth notes** and **bar lines**. Connect the **notes** in **brackets** with a **beam**.

G2   F2   E2   D2   C2   B2   ⌊A2 G2⌋   ⌊F2 G2⌋   C3   A2

⌊A2 G2⌋   ⌊F2 G2⌋   C2   B2   C2   B2   ⌊A2 G2⌋   ⌊F2 G2⌋

E Complete the notes of the second and third octaves with **stems** and **flags**. Name all the **notes**. Circle the **melodic tonic fifth chord** (C, E, G).

Supplemental Educational Material

C Major Scale

Clefi's Little Notebook, pg. 37; Clefi's Music Notebook 1, pg. 9

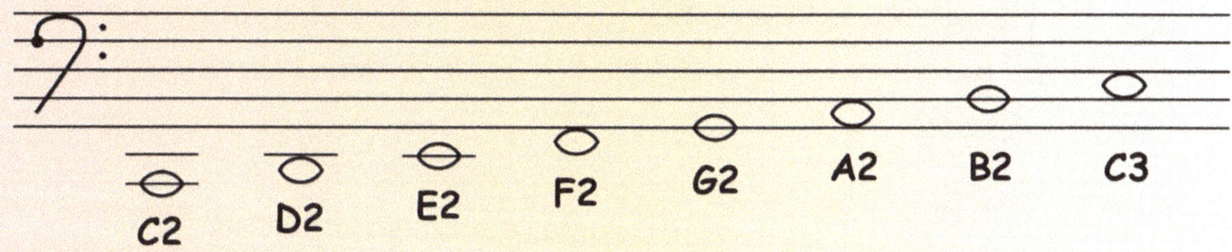

E Using **half notes**, write the **ascending major scale** starting from **C2** in the **bass clef** in **4/4 meter**.

E Write the notes' **names** under the staff. Complete the notes with **stems** and divide the measures with **bar lines** according to the **meter**.

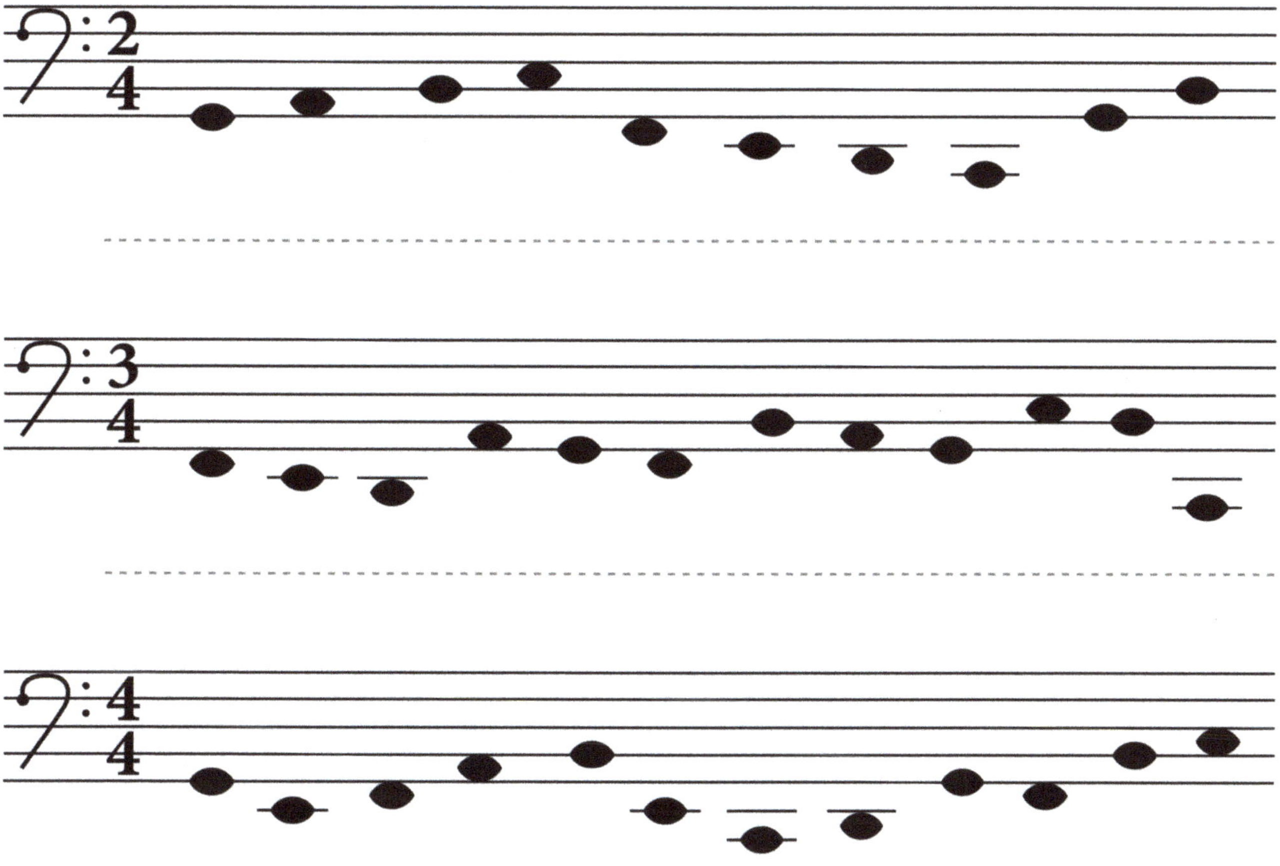

Songs in Second and Third Octaves

E Sing the song "When I Was a Little Boy" from *Clefi's Musical Instrument* on page 30. **Name** the notes in the bass clef transcription below. **Identify** and **circle** the **measure** with the **notes** from the **third octave** in any color.

Clefi & Notelina's Songbook, pg. 27

E Sing the song below using the **names** of the **notes**. **Circle** all the **notes** from the **second octave** in green.

Clefi & Notelina's Songbook, pg. 41

Copy the **measures** from the song above
with the **rhythm** to the right onto the **staff below**.
Do not forget the clef and the time signature.

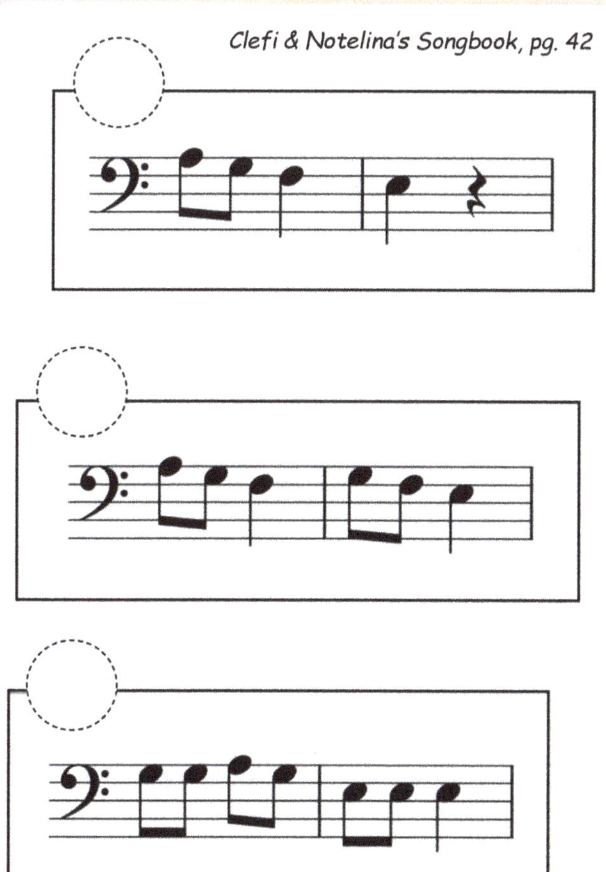

E A beautiful new song was **ripped** into **eight pieces** and **scattered**. We must **number** the individual parts in the **correct order** to put them **back together**. The **first** and the **last parts** are **easy to find** because they have **distinct features**. We also have some details about the parts in between. Are you an excellent **musical detective** who will piece the song back together?

- The **first** part features an important **musical signature**.
- The last, **eighth** part of the song features a **distinct closing bar line**.
- The **second** part contains two measures with notes in the **same descending rhythmic pattern**.
- The **third** part is the **same** as the **opening** part.
- The **fourth** section has the only **rest**.
- The **fifth** and the **sixth** parts are almost the same **except** for the **notes** in their **second** measures.
- The **seventh** section features **two notes**: one from the **fourth** and one from the **third** octave.

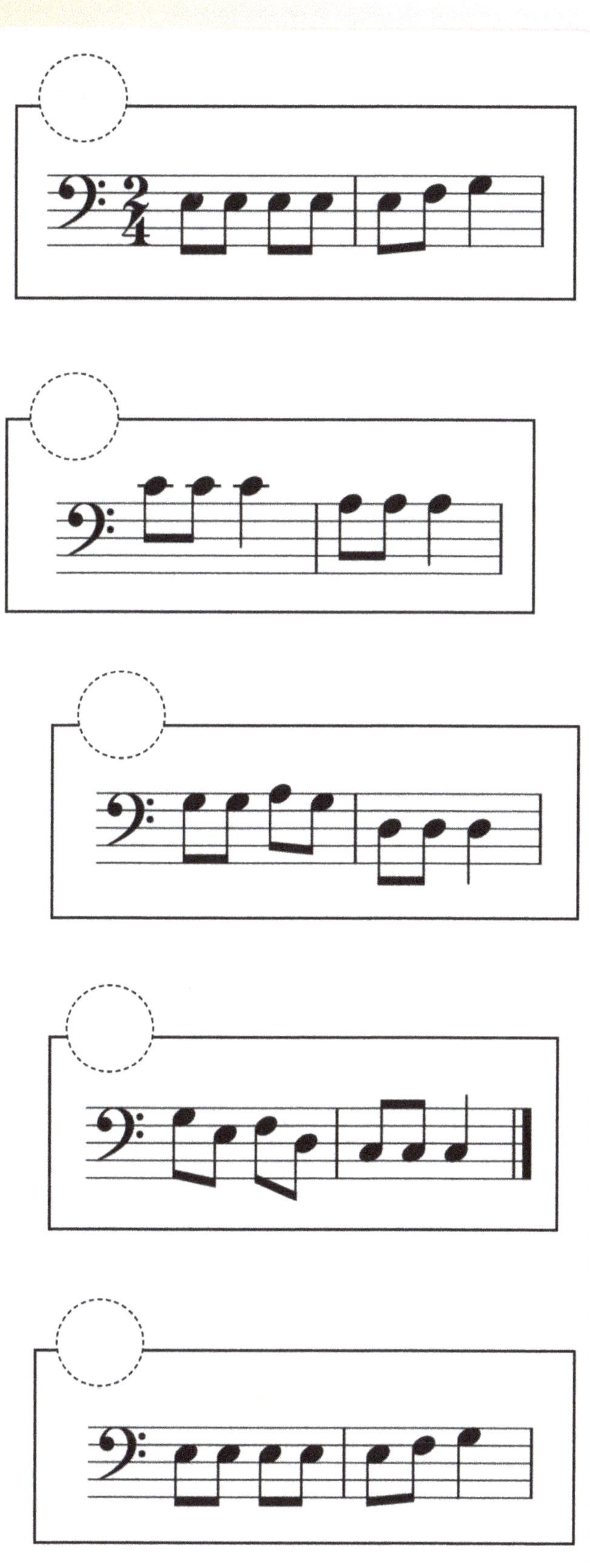

Octave Transposition Symbols

Clefi's Music Notebook 2, pg. 31

When we want the **written notes** to **sound** an **octave higher**, we place the symbol for the **higher octave transposition above them:** *8*--------

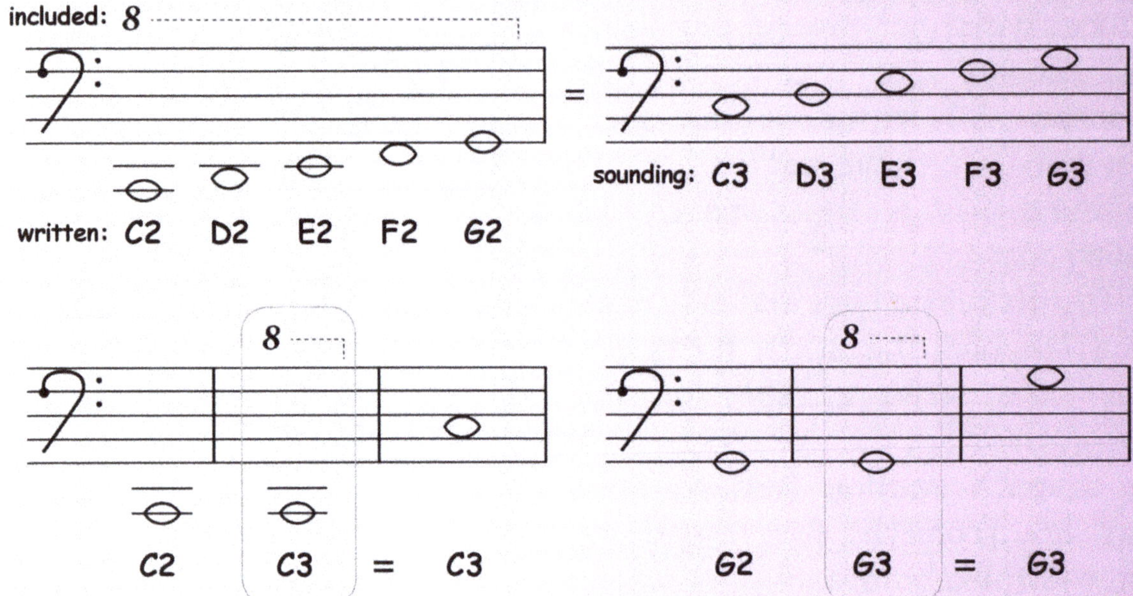

E   Write the **names** of the **notes** on the dotted line below the staff.

E   Name the **notes** on the dotted line below the staff. Mind the **octave transposition symbol** and the **end** of the **bracket** marking its **conclusion.**

When we want the **written notes** to **sound** an **octave lower**, we place the **symbol** for the **lower octave transposition below** them: *8*

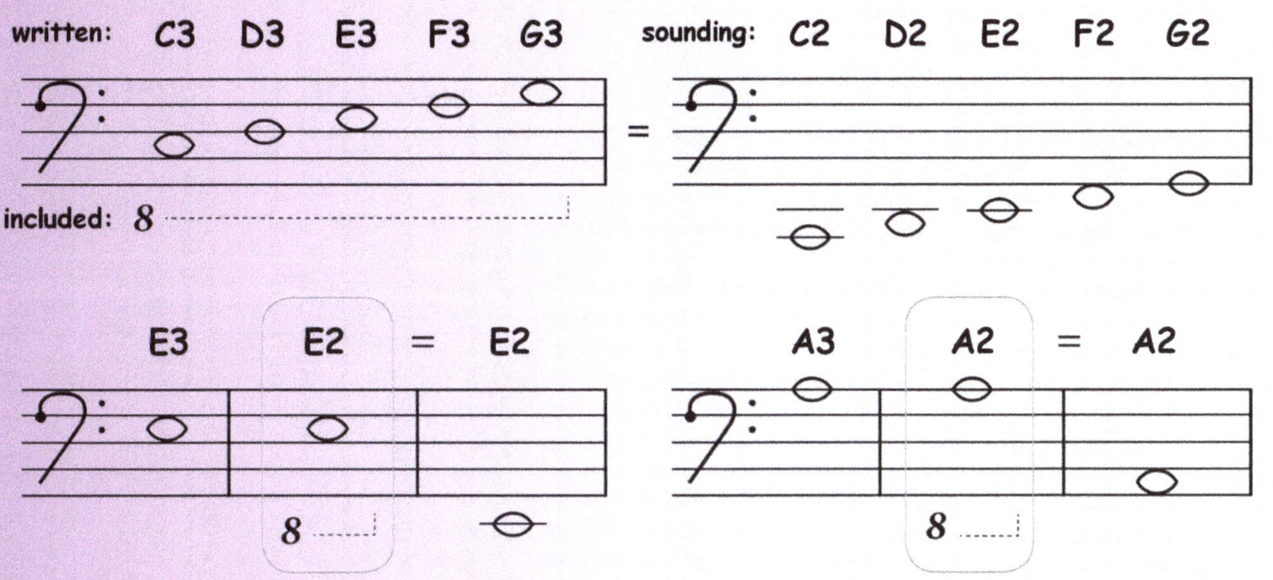

E Write the **names** of the **notes** on the dotted line below the staff.

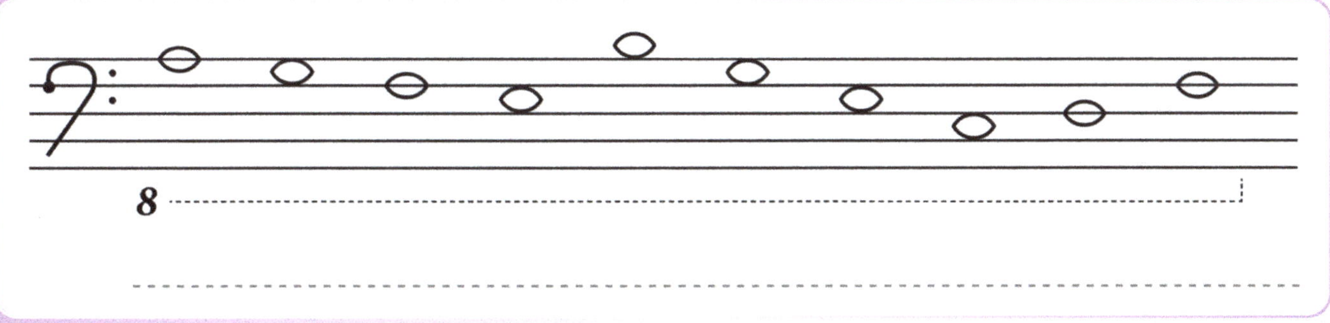

E On the staff below, **copy** the section of the song "I am From a Big, Rich Town" **without** using the **octave transposition symbol**.

Clefi & Notelina's Songbook, pg. 46

C4, D4, E4, F4, G4 in Bass Clef

Clefi's Music Notebook 1, pg. 7

In the bass clef, the **third octave seamlessly links** with the **fourth octave**. The **notes C4** through **G4** are commonly notated in **both clefs**.

In the **treble clef**, the **C4** sits on the **first ledger line below the staff**.

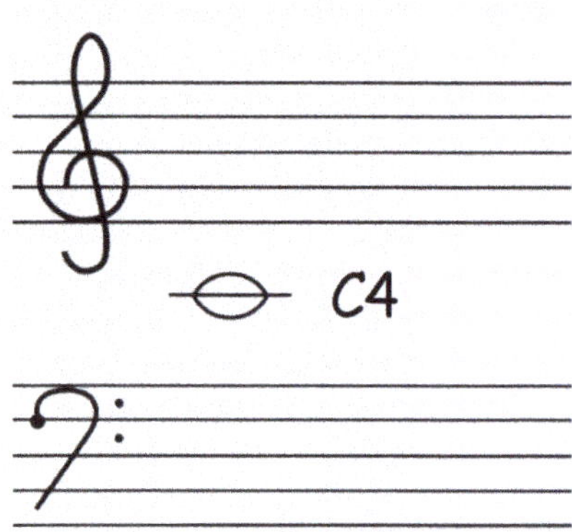

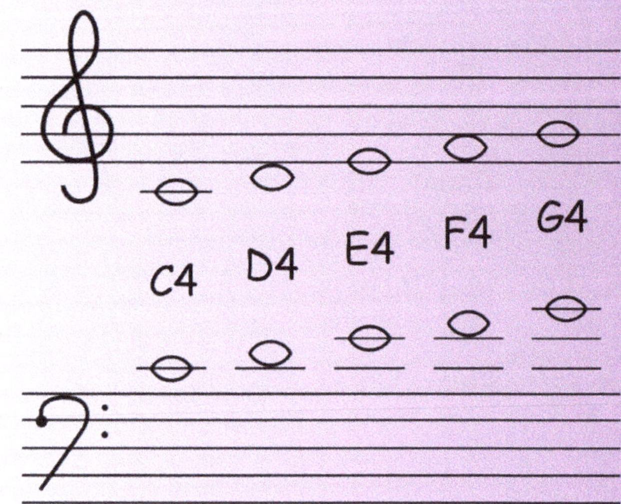

In the **bass clef**, the **C4** sits on the **first ledger line above the staff**.

E | Write the **names** of the **notes** on the dotted line below the staff.

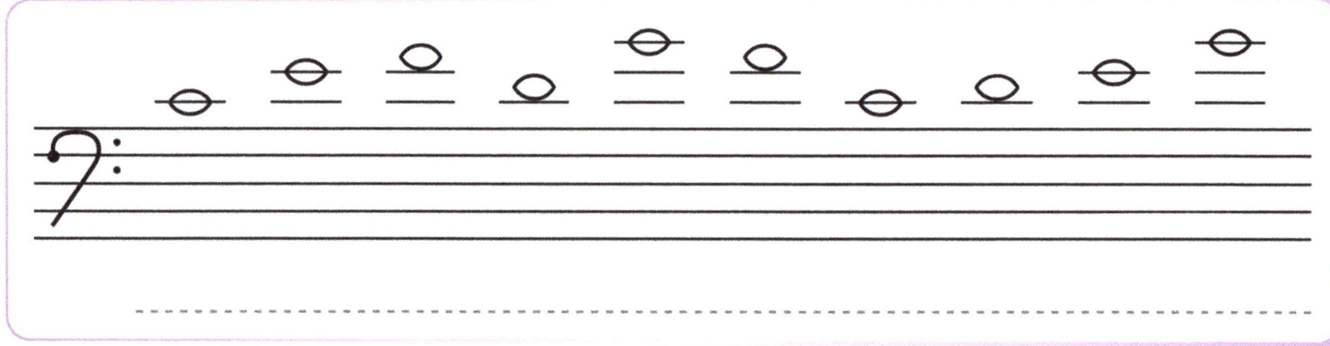

E | Circle the **notes** belonging to the **fourth** octave.

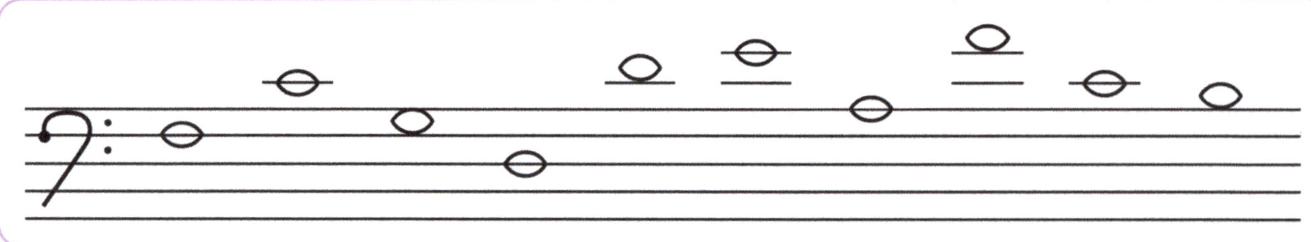

When writing the **notes above** the **staff**, we must pay close attention to the **correct placement** of the **ledger lines**. The **distance between them** must be the **same** as between the **lines** of the **staff**.

E Practice writing the notes **C4** and **E4** in the bass clef. Mind the ledger lines!

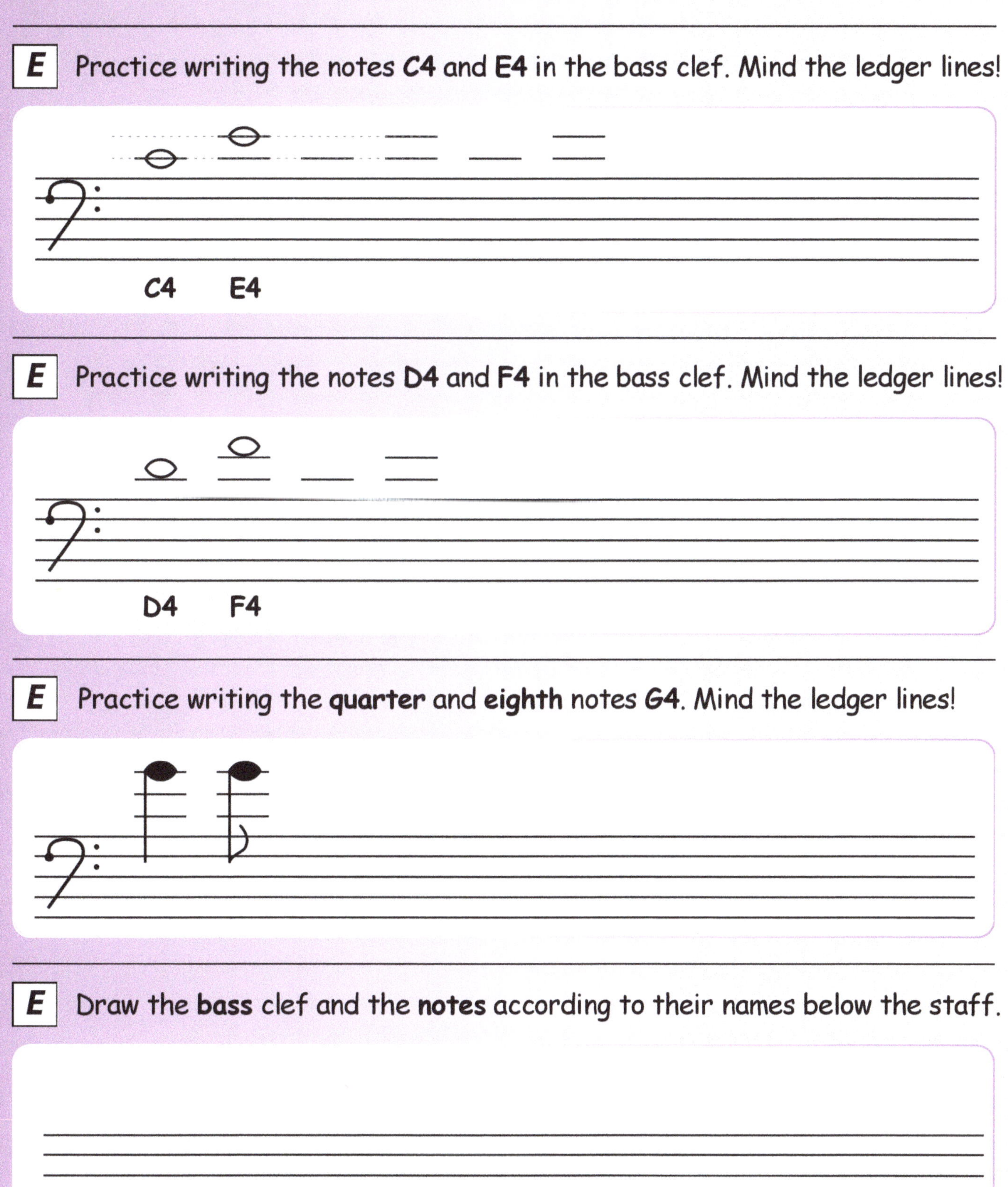

E Practice writing the notes **D4** and **F4** in the bass clef. Mind the ledger lines!

E Practice writing the **quarter** and **eighth** notes **G4**. Mind the ledger lines!

E Draw the **bass** clef and the **notes** according to their names below the staff.

Bass & Treble Celfs

Clefi's Music Notebook 1, pg. 7

At the **beginning** of **every staff**, we write a **clef** that determines the **position** and **pitches** of written **notes**. If we decide to **change** the **clef** in the **middle** of a **piece**, this change is valid until the **end** of the **piece** or until the **next clef change**.

Look at the example of a **double clef change** and how it transitions to the next staff line. *Clefi & Notelina's Songbook, pg. 38*

E Sing the song "A Little Turtle Dove" from Clefi's Songbook at the end of Clefi's Little Notebook (page 60). Write the **names** of the **notes** written in the **bass clef.** *Clefi & Notelina's Songbook, pg. 18*

Big Review

E Color the balloons with the notes ONLY in the **second octave blue** and those with the notes ONLY in the **third octave yellow**. Color the balloons with the **notes** in the **second AND third octaves red**.

E The **eighth notes** from the song "I Am a Musician" from Clefi's Songbook in *Clefi's Little Notebook* (page 61) disappeared. **Fill** them in and **connect** them with the **beams** according to the brackets below the staff.

Clefi & Notelina's Songbook, pg. 20

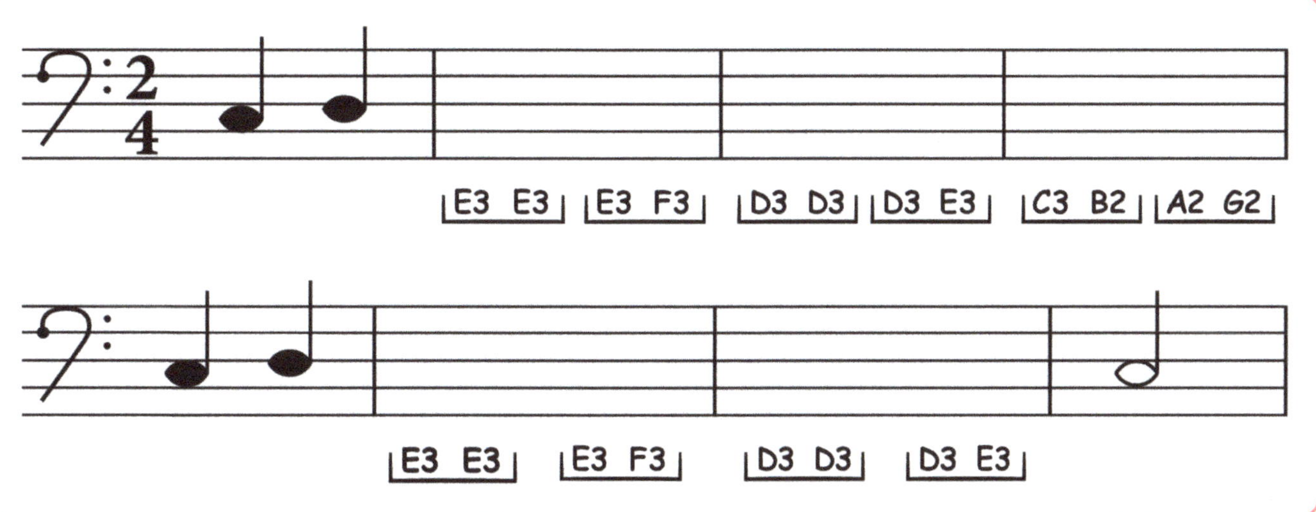

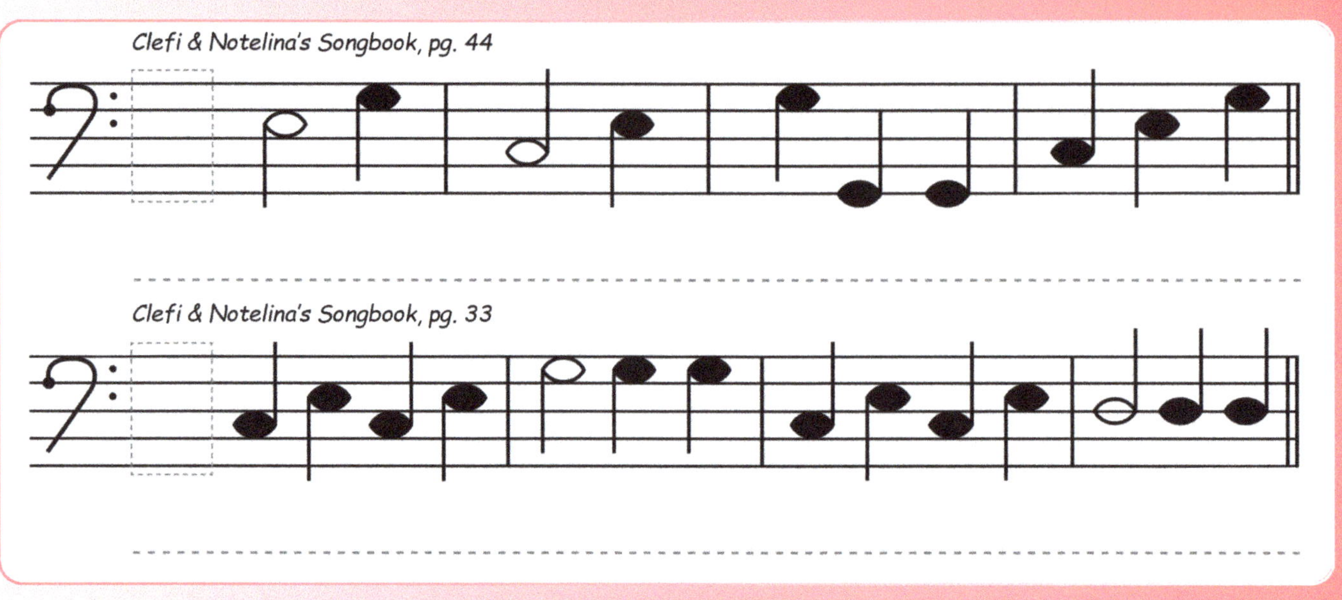

E In the two songs below, fill in the correct **time signatures** and **name** all the **notes** on the dotted lines below the staffs.

E Draw the **bass clef** and write the **notes** according to their **names** below the staff.

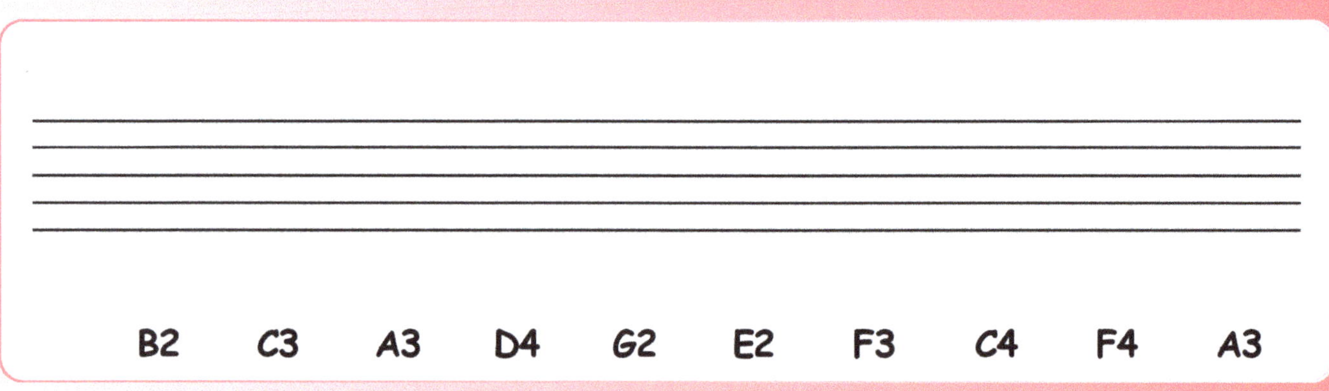

E Copy the measures **without** using the **octave transposition symbols**. Can you name the songs that start with these measures?

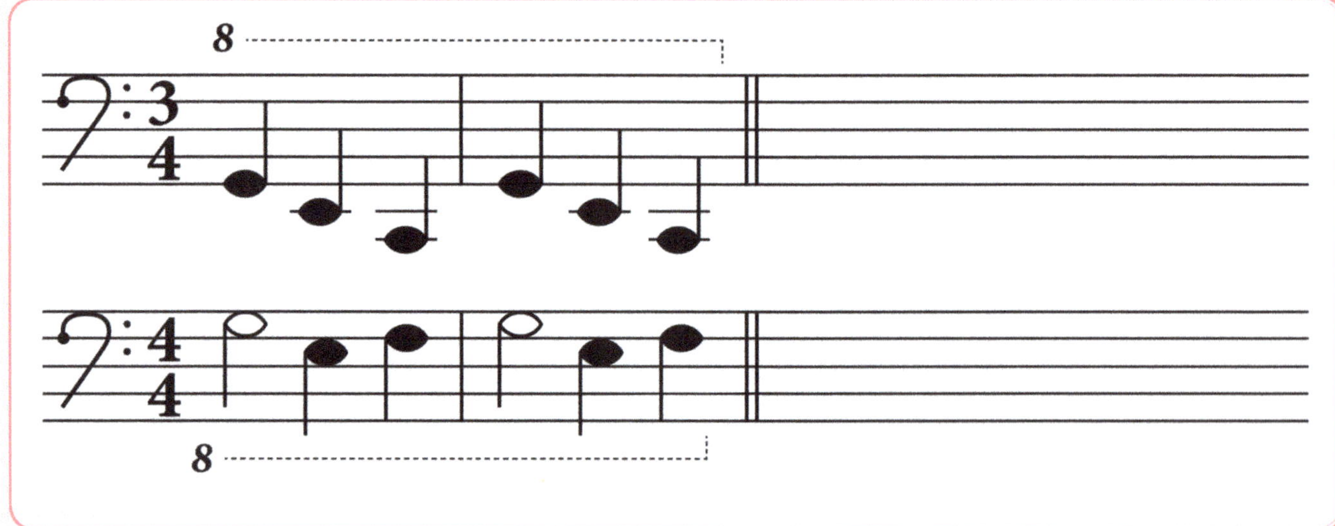

CERTIFICATE

OF COMPLETION

This certificate is presented to:

____

For successfully completing
Clefi's Music Workbook 3

____
music education teacher

Clefi's Little American-British Music Dictionary

Note & Rest Values

Whole note	Semibreve
Whole rest	Semibreve pause
Half note	Minim
Half rest	Minim pause
Quarter note	Crotchet
Quarter rest	Crotchet pause
Eighth note	Quaver
Eight rest	Quaver pause

Note Distances

Whole step	Tone
Half step	Semitone

Octaves

Second octave	Great octave
Third octave	Small octave
Fourth octave	One-line octave
Fifth octave	Two-line octave

Notes

C2-B2	**C-B** (c-b great)
C3-B3	**c-b** (c-b small)
C4-B4	**c'-b'** (one-line c-b)
C5-B5	**c"-b"** (two-line c-b)

Join Clefi's musical family!
Clefi invites you to visit his dedicated webpage and explore the enchanting musical world
of Dr. Eva's New Music Education School Series. Learn more about the author and about
the content of every volume of the series, dive into engaging materials, find answers to
all the exercises, discover more songs, and further deepen your love and understanding
of music and music education. Come make music with us!

www.bumblebeenotes.com/clefis-musical-world

www.bumblebeenotes.com/music-publishing